A Snowy Day

by Robin Nelson

first step nonfiction

It is a snowy day!

The air is cold.

When it is snowy,
the sky looks white.

Snowflakes fall
to the ground.

When it is snowy,
animals leave **tracks.**

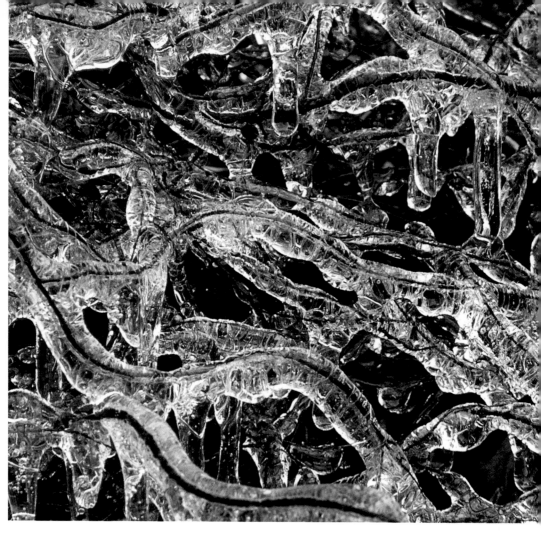

Branches **freeze.**

When it is snowy, snowflakes
melt in our hands.

Snow sticks to our hats.

When it is snowy,
deer **dig** for food.

Birds eat from bird feeders.

When it is snowy,
we wear warm clothes.

We shovel the sidewalk.

When it is snowy,
we make a snowman.

We go **sledding** down hills.

When it is snowy, we warm
our hands by the fire.

A snowy day is fun!

Snowflakes

No two snowflakes are
exactly alike, but each
one has six sides.

Snowy Day Facts

Snowflakes are formed when water droplets freeze in very cold clouds.

Some animals' coats turn white in the winter to help them hide better in the snow. This is called camouflage.

Mount Kilimanjaro is in Tanzania, Africa. The top of the mountain is always covered with snow. The bottom of the mountain is always very hot.

It takes about 50 tiny ice crystals to make one snowflake.

Tamarack, California, holds the record for the most snowfall in one month. In January 1911, 390 inches of snow fell there.

The most snowfall in one winter was on Mount Baker in Washington State. During the winter of 1998–1999, Mount Baker got 1,140 inches of snow.

Glossary

 dig – to move earth

 freeze – to become solid or icy at a very low temperature

 melt – to change from a solid to a liquid because of heat

 sledding – moving over snow in a vehicle

 tracks – marks left by a moving animal

Index

The photographs in this book are reproduced through the courtesy of: © Robert Fried/Robert Fried Photography, front cover, pp. 5, 10, 22 (top); © Richard Cummins, pp. 2, 7, 17, 22 (2nd from top and middle); © Galen Rowell/CORBIS, p. 3; © Stephen Graham Photography, p. 4; © Betty Crowell, pp. 6, 22 (bottom); © bachmann/Photo Network, p. 8; © Eric R. Berndt/Photo Network, p. 9; © Buddy Mays/TRAVELSTOCK, pp. 11, 14; © Rumreich/Photo Network, p. 12; © Beth Osthoff/Independent Picture Service, p. 13; © Richard Thom/Visuals Unlimited, p. 15, 22 (2nd from bottom); © Corinne Humphrey/Visuals Unlimited, p. 16; © Jim Zuckerman/CORBIS, pp. 18 (top left), 19 (top left and top right); © Richard C. Walters/Visuals Unlimited, pp. 18 (bottom), 19 (top center and bottom).

This book is available in two editions:
Library binding by Lerner Publications Company, a division of Lerner Publishing Group
Soft cover by First Avenue Editions, an imprint of Lerner Publishing Group
241 First Avenue North
Minneapolis, MN 55401 U.S.A.

Website address: www.lernerbooks.com

LIBRARY OF CONGRESS CATALOGING-IN-PUBLICATION DATA

Nelson, Robin.
    A snowy day / by Robin Nelson.
        p.   cm. — (First step nonfiction)
    Includes index.
    ISBN 0-8225-0175-9 (lib. bdg. : alk. paper)
    ISBN 0-8225-1964-X (pbk. : alk. paper)
    1. Snow—Juvenile literature. [1. Snow.] I. Title. II. Series.
QC926.37.N45 2002
551.57'84—dc21   00-012945

Manufactured in the United States of America
1 2 3 4 5 6 – AM – 07 06 05 04 03 02